Louis Riel

Terry Barber

ACTIVIST
SERIES

Louis Riel is published by
Grass Roots Press, a division of Literacy Services of Canada Ltd.

PHONE 1–888–303–3213
WEBSITE www.literacyservices.com

ACKNOWLEDGEMENTS

We acknowledge the financial support of the Government of Canada through the Book Publishing Industry Development Program (BPIDP) for our publishing activities.

We acknowledge the support of the Alberta Foundation for the Arts for our publishing programs.

Editor: Dr. Pat Campbell
Image Research: Dr. Pat Campbell
Book design: Lara Minja, Lime Design Inc.

Library and Archives Canada Cataloguing in Publication

Barber, Terry, date
      Louis Riel / Terry Barber.

(Activist series)
ISBN 1–894593–45–6

      1. Readers for new literates. 2. Riel, Louis, 1844–1885.
I. Title. II. Series.

FC3217.1.R53B37 2006   428.6'2   C2006–903724–8

Printed in Canada

Contents

RIEL.

NÉ A LA RIVIERE-ROUGE EN 1847.

MARTYRISÉ A REGINA LE 16 NOVEMBRE, 1885.

Publié par Poirier, Bessette & Cie., Agents de LA PRESSE, Montreal.

Hero or Traitor?

It is November 16, 1885. A man is hanged. His name is Louis Riel. He is hanged for **treason.** Riel is hanged in Canada. Some people think Riel is a hero. Others think he is a **traitor.**

Jean-Louis, the father
of Louis Riel.

Julie, the mother
of Louis Riel.

Early Years

Louis Riel is born in 1844. He is the first child of Julie and Jean-Louis. The Riel family are French **Métis.**

Louis Riel is the oldest of 11 children.

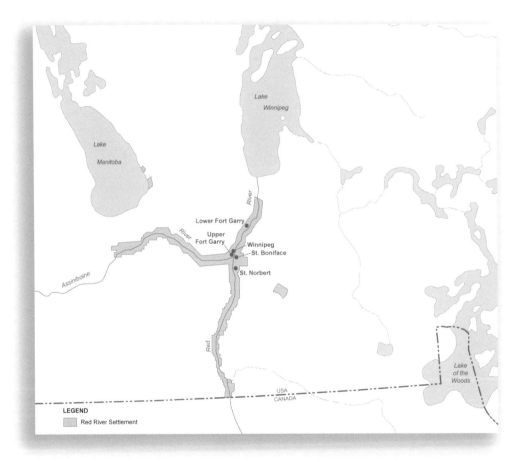

The Red River Colony

Early Years

Riel grows up in Red River. This area is home to almost 12,000 people. Most of these people are **Indians** or Métis. There are French and English Métis.

Most French Métis are Catholic. Most English Métis are Protestant.

The Métis hunters return to camp at Red River, 1859.

Early Years

Some Métis have farms. Some have trap lines. Some hunt bison. Some do all three. By the 1850s, the bison are almost gone. More Métis turn to farming. Métis farmers clear more land.

Louis Riel at age 14.

Early Years

Riel leaves Red River in 1858. He is 13 years old. Riel goes to school in Montreal. He is very smart. Riel wants to be the first French Métis priest.

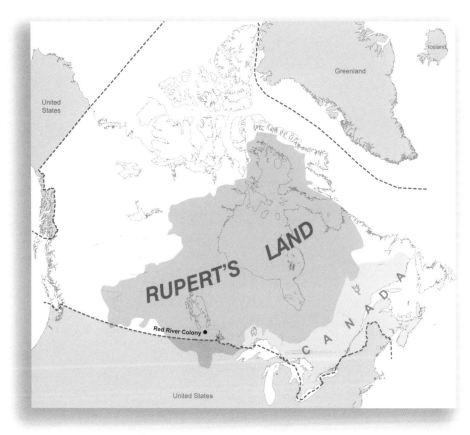

Rupert's Land

Return to Red River

Riel returns to Red River in 1868. Riel returns to unrest. Canada has become a country. Canada wants more land. Canada buys Rupert's Land from the Hudson's Bay Company.

Red River is part of Rupert's Land.

A settler and an Indian.

Return to Red River

Settlers move to Red River. They come from Canada. They speak English. Some settlers do not respect the Métis people. Some settlers want to take control of Red River.

The people who survey the land live in this camp.

Return to Red River

Canada sends people to **survey** the land. The Métis do not have legal title to their land. The Métis fear they will lose their farm land. The Métis ask Riel to be their leader. They want Riel to talk with Canada's leaders.

Riel and his men, 1869.

The Red River Resistance (1869–1870)

The people of Red River elect their own government. Riel is president of the government. Riel and his men get ready to defend Red River. They take over Fort Garry in November 1869. No one is killed.

Riel and his men store food and guns in Fort Garry.

Upper Fort Garry, 1869.

Thomas Scott

The Red River Resistance
(1869–1870)

Riel learns that 48 settlers plan to
attack Fort Garry. The Red River
government arrests the settlers.
Thomas Scott is one of the settlers.
The government orders Scott's death.
Scott is shot on March 4, 1870.

Thomas Scott is shot.

LIST OF RIGHTS.

1. That the people have the right to elect their own Legislature.

2. That the Legislature have the power to pass all laws local to the Territory over the veto of the Executive by a two-thirds vote.

3. That no act of the Dominion Parliament (local to the Territory) be binding on the people until sanctioned by the Legislature of the Territory.

4. That all Sheriffs, Magistrates, Constables, School Commissioners, etc., be elected by the people.

5. A free Homestead and pre-emption Land Law.

6. That a portion of the public lands be appropriated to the benefit of Schools, the building of Bridges, Roads and Public Buildings.

7. That it be guaranteed to connect Winnipeg by Rail- with the nearest line of Railroad, within a term of five years ; the land grant to be subject to the Local Legislature.

8. That for the term of four years all Military, Civil, and Municipal expenses be paid out of the Dominion funds.

9. That the Military be composed of the inhabitants now existing in the Territory.

10. That the English and French languages be common in the Legislature and Courts, and that all Public Documents and Acts of the Legislature be published in both languages.

11. That the Judge of the Supreme Court speak the English and French languages.

12. That Treaties be concluded and ratified between the Dominion Government and the several tribes of Indians in the Territory to ensure peace on the frontier.

13. That we have a fair and full representation in the Canadian Parliament.

14. That all privileges, customs and usages existing at the time of the transfer be respected.

All the above articles have been severally discussed and adopted by the French and English Representatives without a dissenting voice, as the conditions upon which the people of Rupert's Land enter into Confederation.

The French Representatives then proposed in order to secure the above rights, that a Delegation be appointed and sent to Pembina to see Mr. Macdougall and ask him if he could guarantee these rights by virtue of his commission ; and if he could do so, that then the French people would join to a man to escort Mr. Macdougall into his Government seat. But on the contrary, if Mr. Macdougall could not guarantee such rights, that the Delegates request him to remain where he is, or return 'till the rights be guaranteed by Act of the Canadian Parliament.

The English Representatives refused to appoint Delegates to go to Pembina to consult with Mr. Macdougall, stating, they had no authority to do so from their constituents, upon which the Council was disolved.

The meeting at which the above resolutions were adopted was held at Fort Garry, on Wednesday, Dec. 1, 1869. Winnipeg, December 4th, 1869.

List of Rights

The Red River Resistance
(1869–1870)

Riel prepares a list of rights for
the Métis. Riel wins some rights
for the Métis. Canada promises
to give the Métis 1.4 million acres
of land.

Red River
becomes part
of Canada on
May 12, 1870.

THE SCIENCE OF CHEEK; OR, RIEL'S NEXT MOVE.

RIEL (LOQ.)—"FIVE TOUSSAND DOLLARS! BY GAR, I SHALL ARREST ZE SCOUNDREL MYSELF!"

This cartoon shows Riel as a wanted man.

Riel Moves to the U.S.

Some people think Riel is a hero. Others do not. They blame him for the murder of Thomas Scott. There is a $5000 reward for Riel's arrest. He fears for his life. Riel flees to the U.S.

Louis Riel, 1879.

Riel Moves to the U.S.

Riel suffers from stress. He gets sick.
Riel thinks he is a **prophet.** He calls
himself "Prophet of the New World."
Riel's friends commit Riel to a mental
hospital in 1876. He leaves the
hospital in 1878.

Louis Riel in Montana, 1883.

Riel Moves to the U.S.

Riel builds a new life. He teaches school in Montana. He falls in love and gets married. Riel and his wife have two children.

Louis Riel marries Marguerite Bellehumeur on April 27, 1881.

The Métis do not want to live on the Prairies.

The Métis Leave Red River

Canada keeps its promise. Canada gives land to the Métis. The Métis want land on the river. But Canada gives them land on the Prairies. The Métis do not want this land. The Métis sell the land.

The Métis move to the North-West, 1874.

The Métis Leave Red River

In the 1870s, thousands of Métis leave Red River. They move to the North-West. Life is no better in the North-West. The soil is poor. It is hard to farm. The bison are gone. Many Métis die from hunger.

Louis Riel, 1884.

The Métis Leave Red River

The Métis and the settlers want help
from the government of Canada.
In 1884, they meet to choose a leader.
They want Riel to be their leader.
A group of men travel to the U.S.
They ask Riel to return to Canada.
Riel agrees.

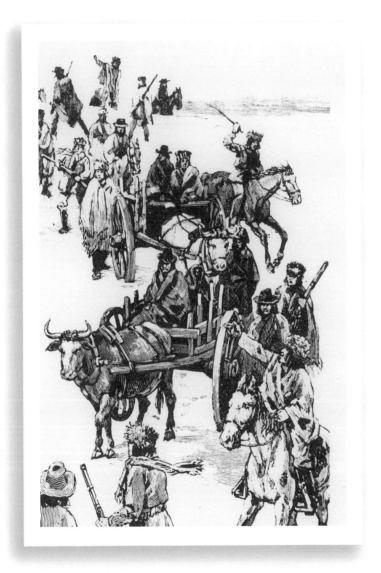

The Métis join the rebellion, 1885.

The North-West Rebellion of 1885

It is December 1884. Riel sends a list of demands to the government. The Indians want food. The Métis want **land grants.** The settlers want lower taxes. Canada does not meet the demands. Some of the Métis leaders decide to use force.

The battle at Duck Lake.

The North-West Rebellion of 1885

The first battle is at Duck Lake. The Métis win the battle. There are more battles. Many people are killed. The last battle is at Batoche in May 1885. It lasts for four days. The Métis lose this battle. The rebellion is over.

Louis Riel is on trial, 1885.

The Trial

Louis Riel turns himself in to the police. Riel is charged with treason. The jury is made up of six men. The jury finds Riel guilty. Riel is hanged.

The men on the jury speak English. They are Protestants.

I have devoted my life to my country. If it is necessary for the happiness of my country that I should now soon cease to live, I leave it to the Providence of my God.

Louis Riel.

The words of Louis Riel.

Riel is Honoured

Today, many people think Riel is a hero. Riel helped win some rights for the Métis. Schools are named after Riel. Streets are named after Riel. Songs are sung about Riel. Books are written about Riel.

Glossary

Indian: Indigenous People in Canada who are not Inuit or Métis. The term First Nations has replaced the word Indian.

jury: a group of 6 to 12 people who make a decision in a court of law.

land grants: a gift of land by the government.

Métis: in the 1800s, Métis means a person of mixed Indian and European ancestry.

prophet: a person who speaks or acts on behalf of God.

rebellion: an open fight against one's government.

survey: to measure land.

traitor: a person who commits treason.

treason: to betray one's country.

Talking About the Book

What did you learn about Louis Riel?

What did you learn about the history
of Canada?

Do you think Louis Riel had a fair trial?
Why or why not?

Do you think Louis Riel is a hero or
a traitor?

Picture Credits

Front cover photos (center photo): © Glenbow Archives NA-504-3; **(small photo):** © Library and Archives Canada, Acc. No. 1982-188-1. **Contents page (top right):** © Glenbow Archives NA-1385-4; **(bottom left):** © Glenbow Archives NA-2631-2; **(bottom right):** © Glenbow Archives NA-710-1. **Page 4:** © Library and Archives Canada, Acc. No. 1982-188-1. **Page 5:** © Library and Archives Canada, Acc. No. C 11 789. **Page 6 (left):** Provincial Archives of Manitoba/N1445; **(right):** Courtesy of the archives of Catholic Family Life Insurance, New England Regional Office, Woonsocket, RI. **Page 8:** © Andreas (Andy) N Korsos, Professional Cartographer, Arcturus Consulting. **Page 10:** © Glenbow Archives NA-1406-8. **Page 12:** © Saint-Boniface Historical Society, Musée de Saint-Boniface collection. **Page 14:** © Andreas (Andy) N Korsos, Professional Cartographer, Arcturus Consulting. **Page 16:** © Glenbow Archives NA-1385-4. **Page 18:** © Glenbow Archives NA-710-1. **Page 20:** © Glenbow Archives NA-1039-1. **Page 21:** © Glenbow Archives NA-1269-2. **Page 22:** © Saint-Boniface Historical Society, Musée de Saint-Boniface collection. **Page 23:** © Archives of Manitoba/N16492. **Page 24:** © Glenbow Archives NA-2929-1. Page 26: © Glenbow Archives NA-3055-12. **Page 28:** © Glenbow Archives NA-504-3. **Page 30:** © Saskatchewan Archives Board R-A5680. **Page 32:** © istockphoto.com/photobarb. **Page 34:** © Library and Archives Canada/C-81787. **Page 36:** © Glenbow Archives NA-2631-2. **Page 38:** © Glenbow Archives NA-1406-241. **Page 40:** © Provincial Archives of Manitoba/ B20/10. **Page 42:** © Saskatchewan Archives Board/R-B1416. **Page 43:** © Glenbow Archives NA-3205-9. **Page 45:** © Glenbow Archives NA-720-2.